Step Up & Grow

Meeting Unexpected Life Challenges at a Higher Level

Susan M. Hansen

Dedication & Thanks

I am dedicating this book to all Step Up Parents, Spouses and family members that choose to step up and help when most people would not.

I thank my many friends that provided different levels of support over the years. I also thank my coach and my friends at Legend Express Publishing for the hour's of guidance and support. The Lions Club that provides many opportunities of service. Finally and foremost, my husband and family who has shared this journey with me.

Introduction

It has been my experience that life will create difficult events and challenges that will help you grow and will mold you into the person you were truly meant to be.

This book was written to encourage others, that when facing a challenge, you can either retreat and give in to the challenge or treat it like a mystery hunt. You don't know where it will lead you, but you may be happily surprised at what you will find, once you are willing to step up and grow.

I was blessed to be raised by some amazing teachers and have had many experiences that gave me a chance to grow into a very strong, compassionate leader early on in life. I was not going to allow any challenge or circumstance knock me down all the way, where I would not be able to get back up.

The following three chapters contain short stories detailing the lessons I have learned along the way. The first chapter contains stories from early childhood up to the age of 18. The second chapter contains stories of exploration and learning the different challenges that come with raising a family. The third chapter contains stories of my later years, with what some consider the golden years. Many people start to get excited about retirement and doing the things they want to do during these years. Now they have the time and financial means to enjoy life at a different level.

I have chosen to leave names and exact dates out of the book for consideration of all parties involved. Through these different life challenges and hidden lessons, I went from an amazing 1.0 version of myself to a 2.0 version which I currently live at. I want to thank my Step-up Dad (my stepdad) who provided some great information and insight while writing this book. I hope by sharing these experiences, you will gain a better insight and appreciation for your life experiences.

Table of Contents

Chapter 1
My First 18 years

Lessons Learned from my Maternal Grandparents

My Maternal Grandparents had a dream, a vision of raising their family in the United States and it only happened after they set this as a goal, created a plan and they were all in to make it happen. Their dream finally happened after they saw an opportunity to immigrate to the United States from Scotland. They packed up the little belongings they had, boarded a ship, said goodbye to other extended family members and came to the United States. They first landed in Canada and stayed with another family member that helped them start the United States Citizenship Process. They knew this would help them get better jobs in their new country to support their family. After some time, they moved on to New York where they set down their roots and finished raising their family. My Grandparents didn't let the fact they had little money or no guarantee for employment stop them from embarking on this journey. They knew this adventure would fulfill their dream of raising their daughters in a country with unlimited opportunity. My Grandfather became a very talented machinist and worked in this profession for many years sharing his talents and gifts with others. My Grandmother went to school and became a very gifted and talented Speech Pathologist. Later, my grandfather was able to get a job working for the Ford Company in Canada and stayed with them until they offered him a position to work for Ford in New York. It was at this job that he met a gentleman "Moog" from MIT that designed the first Servo Motor in his home garage starting Moog Manufacturing in the space and aeronautics business. Moog gained the patent for this and invited my grandfather to come work with him at Moog Manufacturing as a machinist, developing machinery to produce the servo motor. My grandfather gave them many loyal years of service and retired there.

The simple process of setting a goal, getting an education and going to work, set an important model of living for their descendants. They also saw the value of the dollar and the value of having multiple sources of income. They both had a love for reading, exploration and experiencing different things. They loved traveling, meeting new people and adding new experiences. They cruised around the world many times bringing back a lot of teachable experiences to their children, grandchildren and great grandchildren. They lived in many places experiencing different cultures and growing their group of friends. These valuable lessons are still practiced by several of their grandchildren. Their legacy lives on in each of us. I love to travel and have successfully learned how to make Scottish shortbread using a recipe passed down from my grandparents. This is a special treat I still make around the holidays to share with my family. The love of reading and exploration is enjoyed by many of their grandchildren and now great grandchildren.

When my maternal grandmother's health started to decline the decision was made that they would move closer to one of their two daughters. My husband and I with our 3 small sons chose to step up, and move them into our home while they waited for a condo to be built. They were building in a beautiful place, about two hours away in the cooler part of Arizona. Having my grandparents live with us for six months was a fun adventure for all of us. We blended two different age groups of people, that had different life experiences. These were interesting challenges for everyone but a lot of fun. Some of my fondest memories were spent playing scrabble for hours. The hours spent laughing, learning and hearing many stories from their days of travel was a welcomed memory I will always cherish. The move to the Condo finally came and they were able to spend a small amount of time enjoying this new place before my grandmother's health took a severe turn for the worse. They then moved back to town into a place where she could receive the care she needed and still have the freedom to come and go as they pleased.

Thinking back to all the lessons they taught us, the biggest one I have learned is to go after your dream, never giving up regardless of what others say.

Lessons Learned from my Paternal Grandparents

My Paternal Grandmother was a great teacher and taught myself and many others that life may throw a few curve balls, but you must get back up and keep moving towards the things you want in life. Here are some of the other memorable things that she taught myself and many others over the years. My Grandmother experienced several losses over her lifetime. She knew how to celebrate the lives of those closest to her. Her son died as young child, and when I was a very small child, she suffered the loss of another son, my father, in his thirties. She taught myself and many others that it is ok to grieve after the loss of a love one especially the loss of a spouse or child but life must go on. She was fortunate to find love again and married her second husband who we called Grandpa. The two of them experienced many good times together and both shared a love for family. I learned many valuable lessons from them including the love of cooking. They both enjoyed cooking different things but my Grandpa was a very talented Italian cook, making some of the best Italian Food that I have ever tasted. His specialties were Barbeque Hamburgers and Chicken Cacciatore and they were better than any I have ever tasted. My grandmother also had a love for gardening. She grew some of the most beautiful flowers. In addition to spending time in the kitchen we enjoyed laughing and playing card games like Canasta. They also taught me to follow my dreams, enjoy life and spend time with family and friends.

Lessons Learned from Dad

My biological dad who I will refer to as Dad for the simplicity of this book, was a faithful, kind, loving man that didn't mind hard work and had an unconditional love for God and his family, for whom I learned many lessons from.

With the help of my grandfather, Dad was able to gain employment and learn to be a Master Machinist, leading to more opportunity for my parents. He loved working with his hands often creating some beautiful pieces of art, mainly out of wood. He was a very talented craftsman and made several wooden toys for my younger siblings.

His dream was to live and raise his family in the beautiful desert of Arizona. So he along with my Mom packed up their young family of eight, left the security of our family, friends and jobs, and drove out from New York to Arizona to start a new life. I remember this long adventurous drive to Arizona. It was full of many different adventures and unforeseen challenges along the way. Dad drove the moving truck, sharing the ride with either myself or my older sister and one of my younger siblings. Mom drove their only car they had with the four younger siblings including my very active one year old brother that, like most small children didn't like to sit still. Dad was creative and knew this would be an issue. So he built a small play area for my youngest brother to move around in and sleep when he became tired. This cut down on some of the work my older sister and I had since we were assigned the unique challenge of helping with our younger siblings. This six day adventure took us though many states, encountering different challenges along the way. One of my most cherished memories was the personal time with Dad in the moving truck. These were special times. I was one of the older children. My Sister and I were often asked to help out with our younger siblings. We learned some special skills and would not realize the true value of these skills until we raised families of our own.

I value the many lessons he taught me, but the one I cherish the most is the lesson to follow your dreams regardless of what others think. You should not let others decide for you what dreams you should follow.

It was soon after that move, that we would lose Dad from the results of the automobile accident, changing the directional path of our lives along with so many others.

I am happy that he was able to see his dream come true before his untimely death.

Death is the Hardest Lesson to Learn

Another memory from my early years, probably the most memorable one, came while I was in elementary school and occurred during the long hot summer days while living in Arizona. The story I am referring to is the car accident Dad was involved in on the way home from work. This accident eventually cost Dad his life and the carefree life of his family as we knew it back then. When Mom received the phone call to get to the hospital for Dad's accident, we found my youngest brother's blue and lifeless body floating in our swimming pool. Mom immediately pulled him from the water, ran into the house, called the operator (this was before 911 existed) and with the help of the operator learned how to perform CPR, breathing life back into my brother. My older sister helped Mom, I was asked to stay outside and wait for help to arrive at our rural home off the main road in the middle of the desert. The following days after the accident were met with much concern and confusion for many including us children. We were suddenly thrown into a situation where the only thing we knew was that our parents and youngest brother were not around. My brother would recover from his near drowning experience and stay at the home of the pastor and his family. We had many different people come in to help take care of us which was a different experience all together. I remember my mom's sister flying in with her two small children to help out for about a month while my mom went between two different hospitals trying to be there for both my dad and my brother. I am sure this was not easy for anyone as my mom was away from her other children that she loved very much, my aunt stepped up and was soon taking care of five additional children of various ages, including two preteen girls. My aunt's nursing skills came in handy that same summer as my older sister fell off the swing set and broke her arm. My Aunt was able to stay calm and get my sister the medical attention she needed. It is my understanding that my Dad's injuries would require many surgeries, and many pints of blood during his month long stay in the hospital. At this time, Mom and other friends and family would need to donate blood so Dad would have the necessary supply he needed to survive. It was during one of the many surgeries that he would go into cardiac arrest. After a long courageous fight, Dad succumbed to his injuries.

This next tragic story comes from blurred memories but with such a profound impact it must be told. Some of the details were relayed from other family members.

It was on one simple, hot summer day that tragedy once again challenged our family, strengthening us in a way most people would not think possible. The story is about my two younger brothers that were full of energy and excitement. They just earned some extra money and were riding their bikes to the local corner store to buy some candy. They were racing each other across the street in the crosswalk, when a car, blew through the intersection against the light hitting both brothers. The older of the two brothers was winning and took the brunt of the impact, receiving the most injuries. The youngest brother came around with a police officer bending over him, rendering aide. He was transported to the hospital in the back of the police car. The oldest brother's injuries were so severe he was transported the short distance to the hospital on top of the fire truck, not waiting for the ambulance. It was after arriving at the hospital and after much testing it was determined his injuries were too severe for him to survive. My younger brother's injuries were less severe and he would make a full recovery physically. The death of my brother would inspire me to be able to continue to compete and be the best I could be in spite of challenges.

Lessons Learned from Mom's New Life

Mom was a strong courageous lady and was now faced with a unique situation that she must find a solution for. Now a young widow, with six kids that she was responsible for and no job or formal education that would provide for the growing needs of her family. Mom knew her new life would be challenging, but she chose to step up. Trade school provided the best option to obtain her Certified Nursing Assistant Certificate (CNA).

Mom had a strong will and perseverance to succeed at anything she set her mind to. If and when someone would tell her that something could not be done, she would quietly get to work and either find or create a solution to prove her point. All things are possible if you set your mind to it. One particular time I remember was the sudden and unexpected move from my parents dream home out in the beautiful desert situated amongst the different plants and cacti came suddenly and with little warning at least for us kids. It was soon after the passing of Dad, I remember coming home from school. Mom had the car packed, told us to get in the car and don't ask any questions. I could tell from the expression on her face that we should just do what she asked and get in the car. I found out years later that this sudden and unexpected move came as a result of a busy body neighbor that thought Mom should be doing things different. We were giving up this peaceful and tranquil lifestyle and moving to an apartment closer to town so Mom could finish her CNA education. This was a profession my mom found she enjoyed and would be the answer to how she would support her family of seven. Mom had to work so my younger siblings went to daycare and my sister and I took care of ourselves after school until she finished work. When Mom got home, my older sister and I would take care of our younger siblings and learned how to cook so she could take care of other things like pay bills and make sure there was enough money for food and other things. My older sister and I had to step up because there were little services available to help low income families at this time.

She first learned about the American Red Cross and some of the many services they offer while Dad was in the hospital. Mom was not afraid of hard work. This was the beginning of a long relationship with the American Red Cross that would last up until her later years when her health didn't permit her to live on her own. It was part of Mom's mission in life to help others wherever or whenever she could. She had friends all over the world so when she was offered the chance to work with FEMA she jumped at it. With Mom's love for adventure and her passion for helping others, she was often away from home, traveling the world to different disaster sites. She was always ready and willing to go at a moment's notice often taking her away from her family that she loved so much.

Mom lived by this moto, "There was no challenge too small, as long as you have the desire and means to accomplish it." She taught me the most about life, about hard work, and the value of setting goals and never giving up.

Lessons Learned from Step-up Dad

This next story is about second chances for two amazing people, the courtship between Mom and Step-up Dad, my step-up dad and the blending of two families. This story begins when the pastor and his wife knew that they would have to use encouragement and creativity, to help a young widow and her children. They came over one evening, put my mom in the car, gave her the instructions to attend a meeting that was being held by a group, "Parents without Partners," and sent her on her way. They also took on the brave task of taking care of her six children, so she could go out and have some time with other adults and hopefully some enjoyment. It was through this group that my mom met a young father, recently divorced, doing his best to raise his young son and daughter. It was after this first meeting they decided they wanted to get to know each other more so they started dating. After a short period of time they introduced us children to each other. This took place at the biggest ocean in the middle of the desert, BIG SURF, and began a lifetime friendship between us siblings. With the help and encouragement of Step-up Dad, Mom moved into town where she was close to work and other services. This big move came quick and with little notice, as I mentioned earlier. I remember asking her what about our friends and my reading glasses that I left at school. Her response was very simple, "We will get the glasses replaced, get into the car and don't ask any more questions." I knew by the tone of Mom's voice that we better just do what she said. So we did.

After a short courtship, they knew they wanted marriage. They flew to Las Vegas and got married, blending these 2 families together to make it one strong, loving family of ten. Of course we all got along well....

Step-up Dad was an amazing leader and teacher. He taught us the true meaning of a strong family and love for adventure. When he married Mom, he committed to take on 6 additional children all different ages, dealing with the death of their father. My older sister and I were just getting ready to enter the awkward teenage years. I can safely say it was not an easy task of raising teenagers, but he stayed committed to Mom and to our family for which I am forever grateful for. This wonderful patient man made sure we continued going to church, taught us how to drive our cars, and many other lessons along the way. He also helped all of us work through the death of one brother while helping another brother recover from his injuries that he sustained in the same accident. My family found much comfort from our pastor and many others including neighbors.

Our new blended family had many adventures. We would pile into an old pickup with a camper and take a road trip, usually to California to visit family. Step-up Dad even honored Mom's wish and drove our family on a three-month road trip along the Atlantic Coast, to Florida to visit Disney World and ultimately finishing in New York so we could see extended family. He was also there for all of us to lean on when we received the sudden and unexpected news that two of my younger brothers were hit by a car. He taught me how change the oil and do simple maintenance on our old cars. He walked me down the aisle when I married the love of my life right after high school.

As you can see he really is a Step-up dad and will always will be.

Lessons Learned in the BIG House

Another story was moving to the big house as we called it. After my brother's untimely death and a decline in the neighborhood we moved to a large 5 bedroom 4 bath home with a large kitchen, family room, above ground pool and many other amenities including a large fire place. This house sat on a quarter acre which was large enough, so the multiple animals could run free. Mom loved animals, but her biggest passion was dogs of all sizes. We at one time had three Great Danes that ran freely around the property, they also made great guard dogs. We had many great memories at this house that included multiple swim parties, sleep overs and other get-togethers with family and friends. This was where my oldest sister and I had our wedding receptions.

In this house we learned to heal and celebrate life. Change gives you the best opportunity to learn new relationships and overcome challenges.

Chapter 2
Being Together is Awesome

Lessons Learned from Love

I will begin this next chapter with a beautiful love story between two young people that made a choice to follow their hearts. It is the love story of my husband and myself in which I will share some particular insight. So please sit back and enjoy.

This story starts with a young man, the young son of a minister that met the girl of his dreams at a church social event. He was eighteen and I, was a young girl of fifteen. He finally got out of his shell and made the first phone call. This began the dating process and the building of an incredible relationship. The first date came one evening when he asked me out to the movies. After receiving permission from my parents,

I was able to accept the offer. The date and time were set. I was excited, but full of different emotions as the day approached. This being my first date with "A BOY WITH A CAR" made me nervous. I didn't know what to expect and many different things rolled around in my mind. I even remember telling myself to relax and stop being nervous. I was just going out to the movies and was not going to marry this boy.

The day soon came. I spent the day getting ready and finally he came to pick me up. On the drive to the movies, we talked and I soon relaxed allowing myself to have a great time. The days following this date, I couldn't get this boy out of my mind. When he called to ask me out again, I said "yes" without hesitation. I soon realized that I wanted to spend as much time with this boy as my parents and time would allow. We decided to become "boyfriend and girlfriend," and soon spent the weekends together, going out to movies or just spending time together exploring life and building our relationship. A few years later, no surprise to anyone, this boy proposed. The proposal was unique to us and was very simple. We knew we wanted to spend the rest of our lives together, so we went to the jewelry store, picked out a ring and after placing the ring on my finger I knew that he was committed. We held off a few days before sharing our engagement with family and friends. He wanted to see if anyone would notice the ring. I have a hard time keeping secrets so the next few weeks we shared the engagement with our friends and families and set the date for the wedding. This gave us a year to plan for the perfect day.

The big day finally came after much excitement and planning. The wedding took place on a beautiful warm evening at the church where we originally met and held so many great memories. In front of family and friends, the groom's father (a Minister) and the pastor of the church officiated this beautiful union. The ceremony started with a large wedding party leading the procession, consisting of the Flower Girl dressed in a long beautiful powder blue gown tossing ever so slightly small peddles onto the ground walking beside the handsome Ring Bearer decked out in a tan tuxedo, followed by the Junior

Bridesmaid, three additional Bridesmaids and the Maid of Honor all dressed in long powder blue dresses. The two Ministers then came out of a side door followed by the handsome Groom himself, dressed in a white tuxedo, five Groomsman and Best Man all looking amazing in tan tuxedos. Now the moment everyone was waiting for. Music was playing in the background and I, dressed in a long beautiful white gown with a long white train flowing on the ground made my entrance. I was escorted slowly down the aisle holding onto the arm of the brave man that married Mom many years before. The short but beautiful ceremony included a beautiful song, sung by friends of the family, and the reading of scriptures. It culminated with the groom lifting the veil off my face, then reciting of the wedding vows to each other and the lighting of the Unity Candle. We finally led the procession out of the church to greet the many family and friends that came in from different parts of the world, to witness our beautiful union.

The reception that followed took place in my parent's large spacious back yard, in the BIG HOUSE. Dining on a simple spread of sandwiches, among many trays of different fruits and vegetables for the guests to choose from. There was dancing to music played on a jukebox, people laughing and having a great time. This was the wedding I had dreamed of. This was followed by a honeymoon in a remote cabin a short two hour drive from where we would start or new life together.

The first two years as a young married couple was fun, full of different adventures and challenges to say the least. I was the second oldest coming from a large family, full of knowledge and experience in raising my siblings. My husband was the youngest child of a family of eight. I had a desire to go to trade school and get into the workforce with full time employment. It was my husband's desire to help me make this happen. So, my husband went back to his full-time job while I settled into school. This was quite an adjustment for me as I was always helping take care of my younger siblings and never gained any study habits. I finally successfully completed my goal and graduated from the school. I found a full-time job that I enjoyed and worked there until we would start our family.

Lessons Learned from Starting a Family

This next story is about purchasing our first home. It was our goal, like many couples to be settled in a home before welcoming any children into the family. We started the hunt for our perfect first house. It was not long after that we found the perfect home with a short commute to my husband's place of employment. This large four bedroom, two bath home with a small but spacious kitchen, a large dining area, and a modern front room. There was a large grass yard in the front. There was a large mulberry tree in the corner of the back yard that would be a perfect place for a future tree house for a growing family. This purchase was made and finalized right before we would welcome the first of our three sons. This was not an easy task but it was our goal to be in a house before we welcomed children into the family.

It was years later that we would be forced to test the part of our wedding vows, "In times of sickness and health." This is where I will begin the last and final chapter three.

Lessons Learned from Aging Parents

This next story is the loss of an amazing, caring, friend and parent. Mom was a lady that loved helping people and life itself. This was Mom's mission in life, to help others wherever or whenever she could. She had friends living though out the world and loved helping others and being with her family. Mom loved the thrill of adventure and when disaster struck she would be the first one ready and willing to respond on a moment's notice. If and when someone would tell her that something could not be done, she would quietly get to work and either find or create a solution to prove her point, that all things are possible if you set your mind to it.

When she started having memory issues we knew something was wrong. She had homes in 2 different states and would travel when and wherever she was needed the most, which prevented us from getting a medical diagnosis.

I remember the call that came one early morning from my sister relaying the message that Mom had fallen and broke her hip. My husband and I flew out that day and were picked up by one of her neighbors and brought to Mom's house before heading to the hospital to spend time with Mom. We also knew after spending a few hours with her that we were dealing with much more than a broken hip. She didn't remember the fall or that she had hip surgery. She would try and tell me she had surgery on something else. I reported my findings back to my siblings and went back to her place and visited with her neighbors. We soon found out that there were several instances that brought concern to the neighbors, but they had no way of contacting any of her children since Mom kept that information from them. She would tell us that she had given our contact information to her neighbors in case of emergency but actually did not. The neighbors found the information after my mom's fall and contacted us right away. It was decided after my visit that we would contact her doctors and get some additional testing done on her memory to see if it was safe for her to live on her own. It was determined that she was in the early stages of Alzheimer's and we needed to act quickly to get her moved to a safe place in the state that she loved, Arizona. The move took the help of many of us and occurred within a few weeks after the fall. My younger brother flew to her home, packed up her things, and drove her back to her family in Arizona. While he was dealing with this, my older sister and I were locating a safe facility for her to move into.

My siblings and I are grateful for the kind neighbors that took notice of Mom's condition and went through great effort to locate our contact information. I wish we could have been there to help her more, but she always declined help, it was just in her nature. I wish I could have had the courage of our Pastor and told her to "Shut up and get in the car." I hope that I'll listen to my children when that day comes.

Chapter 3
Believing in Myself

Lessons Learned In Times of Sickness and Health

This next test would come around 20 years into our union and after working through many challenges and obstacles as a couple. The test started with one phone call from my strong, husband that shared a belief with his father and so many other husbands that, "it was his responsibility to work and provide for his family." I remember when the call came from my husband. He let me know that he didn't feel good and needed someone to come and get him, since he didn't feel safe to drive home. We were fortunate that our sons were willing and able to step up and help get him home. They continue helping along with other family members, since we know there is no cure for my husband's health challenges. His condition removed his ability to provide for his family at the level he would like to.

We are blessed and grateful for our sons as they have offered us help, even though they are looking for ways to handle their own unexpected challenges like paying for college.

I was at work about 45 minutes away and was still in a probationary position. Not wanting to jeopardize my job and knowing that our two sons, both teens and drivers, were at home and had access to a vehicle. I called them to explain the situation and asked them to step up and while one would go get their father, the other one stayed home and watched over his younger brother. After getting home and accessing the situation, I started making phone calls and setting up appointments to look for answers about my husband's health. This long process extended over years. We were dealing with a sort of a mystery.

Several years later, after meeting a ninety-two-year-old man, we had some answers. He stepped up and shared some information about new breakthroughs and other possibilities available. We looked at the reports, checked with doctors, and found that this would not hurt or interfere with his medications. We understood there is no cure for the health challenges that would plague my husband, at least our family had hope with the occasional small bursts of energy that he could enjoy time with us again. The results we started seeing after a short few months gave us a new hope. Over time we have been able to make changes to our life style and start planning for the future.

It was several years later that we as a family would be given another challenge and opportunity to step up. This came after a routine checkup and additional testing that my husband would be diagnosed with Cancer. This news brought many different emotions for many of us. It also gave us time to reflect and offered others the opportunity to step up and spend valuable time with my husband while I was out taking care of things away from the home front. We are happy to report at the time of this publication my husband is cancer free.

The next challenge we faced was how we would handle the large amount of mounting medical bills. We found the amount of loss is different for everyone but in our case, some of the insurances and investments we put in place fell short when the economy took a hit around 2009. Out of pure drive and determination and with the mindset of "never giving up," I went to work. My husband was not able to help much since his illness has many disabling side effects. Most of the work was by me. I spent hours filling out mounds of paperwork, evaluating the budget, adjusting and making other important decisions on what areas we could make cutbacks in including using the college fund we were saving for since we started or family. I also started looking for additional employment options that I could make money and work from home. I needed something that had flexible hours since I was the main caregiver for my husband. My sons were willing to make sacrifices and help were ever they could, but it was my decision to take on most of the work load, so they could continue with their lives.

I am grateful for the valuable economizing lessons I learned as a child including the ability to cook and prepare meals of all sizes. I still cook in mass volume and divide the left overs in different proportions to freeze for later enjoyment. We have enjoyed many meals with family and friends with the food I prepared and froze on one of my less busy days where I can spend time in the kitchen.

I had to ask myself, "What I am going to do now? How I am going to meet our financial commitments with the loss of my husband's salary and the medical costs associated with his health challenges?" These were the real life questions I had to ask myself since this was the first time we had experienced such a financial hit. I kept my options open when looking for a 3rd job. This turned out to be more challenging than I thought. I needed something with flexible hours and with no college degree required. I needed something that allowed me the freedom to be there for my husband's medical appointments and other things I needed to do in being the primary care giver in our home. I started looking for this additional source of income around 2009 and found it in 2012.

I am forever grateful for the opportunity I was given to have met that same incredible ninety-two-year-old gentleman and his slightly younger wife. I was at their home, testing out my skills by selling knives. This couple introduced me to an industry that I knew very little about. The Network Marketing industry can be very profitable and fun if you find the right fit. I liked the nutritional products they offered and the residual income program. The products made a big difference in my husband's health and we would be using them for the rest of our lives, so I thought why not. I jumped in with both feet. This was the start of a new journey that would lead me to meet some extraordinary people among other things. I still enjoy the many benefits that go along with this choice including the improved health and many friends I have acquired over the years.

The third and final lesson in this chapter I would like to share is the lesson that comes with drive and perseverance. The high cost that most families encounter when attempting to take care of a loved one with health challenges can lead to depression and other health issues for the caregiver. This emotional, mental, physical and the other cost is more than monetary and other effects, not only for the couple but many of their family members as well. You can attempt to prepare for such challenges but there is no amount of preparation that could prepare a family for this situation. I have two suggestions to offer regarding this. Number one. Don't judge, each family's experience is different. Number two. If you or your loved ones are experiencing something like this currently, know you are not alone and others are willing and able to step up all we must do is ask.

I remember my husband as a hard worker and very handy around the house. Seeing him in this situation has been hard to cope with. Learning to persevere through these circumstances, has been a real character building experience. I embrace, accept, and love these new challenges and the new way I feel about myself and my life.

Lessons Learned from New Discoveries

This next story is about a middle age lady that wanted something more out of life. Not knowing what I wanted more of, but something "more." The journey in finding out what this "more" was, unleashed something in me that I never knew existed. This is part of my story of who I truly am and some hidden discoveries I made along the way.

I made the choice a few years back to step out of corporate America and step up to the challenges and adventures of overseeing my time and financial security. I currently enjoy multiple sources of income from a variety of opportunities that I found to be most helpful and a lot of fun. Keeping an open mind and looking at other options, opens the doors of opportunity. This door opened for me and gave me the chance to leave my corporate job and venture into this new territory. After discussing and working through my options, a plan was made, and a new horizon came into view. This choice made me feel happy and free. I could be ME! The fear of the unknown can be scary but if you take a calculated leap of faith, you are in control of the results.

The first curve-ball we faced were some of our insurance resources that we were depending on went away with little to no warning. I had to revisit my personal "Why," the reason I was doing what I was doing, to find the perseverance to continue. When I remembered this, I found new energy and resources to push on. I wanted the freedom and the challenges that went along with owning my business and I was not turning back no matter what curve-ball was thrown my way. This is the reason why I did not go back into the work place after our income sources thinned out.

Lessons Learned from Persistence

The transformation and retirement of the 1.0 version to the 2.0 version has been quite a journey. The journey started when I said yes to a training program with a coach that would help me get out of my own way and get what I was truly after, "more." I had to first retire the 1.0 version that focused on putting everyone else first and create the 2.0 version of myself where I put my wants and desires first. This has been an experience and journey that I am forever grateful to have been on.

It started when a coach telephoned me out of the blue and shared some information about a program that would help me find the missing piece to the puzzle and get me where I wanted to go. I did what I have always done before making a serious decision like this, I asked my husband to join in the phone call and ask some questions, so we could make a more informed decision. What I didn't expect was the reaction that my husband would display. He asked one important question, "Can you help my wife get unstuck?" He must have liked what he heard because my husband's response was, "yes she will sign up for the program that was being offered." This caught me totally off guard, but I will be forever grateful that my husband stepped up and confirmed my decision for me. This single decision helped me unleash what I commonly refer to as a hornet's nests. This nest was full of mixed emotion and held the missing key to the puzzle or as most will put it "my true purpose in life, 'more.'"

I knew I had the love and support of my husband and boys, but I also didn't know where the financial resources would come from. I knew I needed this coach and program. It would change my life. Just as if a son or daughter needed a lifesaving procedure, I knew this was that important to me and that this financial burden would become my lifesaving support line.

I encourage others to step up and start planning financially by putting even just a small amount away for the future. There is no guarantee that this will be enough if or when the time comes where you will need it, but you don't know until you need it.

The transformation started to be unleashed after working with my coach, teacher and mentor. This program changed the direction and path, uncovering so many beautiful things I didn't know existed. When I began, I was frustrated, unhappy, and felt lost. Not knowing why, but I needed something to change. What I didn't know was that I could have so much more while still taking care of my husband and the home front. All I had to do was give myself permission to put my needs first, before others and stop listening to the naysayers. This had to happen both at the emotional and physical level. I had to do some deep soul searching. Some would say, "looking deep down inside yourself." I just didn't know what I wanted or how I was going to get it until I said "yes" and started working on it.

Six months later, I knew I was on the right path, I felt full of joy, gratitude, feeling like I was becoming a new person, a person that I had not known for many years. I felt like I was given a second chance in life to go exploring while enjoying the blessings of a great family. I found myself laughing and peaceful. I have always been a firm believer that things happen for a reason, we may not always understand at the moment it is happening, but there is a reason behind the directional path you are on. I have always known our minds are a powerful tool that will help lead us to the path you need to be on. What I didn't understand was that until I relaxed, and allowed my mind to go exploring different path's, I would be stuck at the 1.0 version.

I set a goal of what I wanted, not what someone else wanted, but what I wanted. I put this on paper, along with some affirmations and went to work. The 1.0 version was also attempting to run a business that was not producing the success I was looking for, while I was still taking care of my husband and the home front. I found that putting my wants first for even just a small window of time, put me in a much happier place with more energy, joy and gratitude. Especially on the days I usually didn't allow myself this luxury. I must admit, not everyone was happy with my transformation, and that was ok with me. Through this course that I found that I was lying to myself for many years. I could have so much more when I planned, put in the work and didn't look back.

I am and will always be a compassionate daughter, sister, wife, mom and grandmother that enjoys spending time taking care of the home, and my husband. This is what gives me happiness.

Lessons Learned from Helping Others

The upgraded version of the new me, the 2.0 version found I like to bake and cook a multitude of different things, but I no longer enjoyed spending hours in the kitchen cooking and baking and then dealing with the cleanup. In addition, I discovered I still enjoyed crocheting and creating different things. I found that when I was making it just for fun, verses making it at the request of someone that wanted to possibly purchase the item, I completed the project at a much faster rate. I came to a better understanding of WHY this was happening. I have never wanted to make money off anything I crochet, rather I enjoy seeing the smiles on the person's face that I created the gift for. It was with this discovery that I decided to write out an affirmation, "I am so happy and grateful now to see the smile on the recipients face when I deliver a gift." I made a decision after this discovery that I would only allow others to purchase the yarn for a requested item, and make sure

I followed my original thoughts that I would never go into the business of making items to put up for sale. If I didn't feel like I wanted to give this as a gift, I would thank the person and decline the request. It is amazing how life provides the answers we need. All we have to do is be willing and able to listen. This is one of the most profound self-discoveries I came across after I gave myself permission to hire a coach to help me explore why my business wasn't going in the direction I wanted it to go. Another discovery I found as part of creating the 2.0 version of myself is I no longer cared what others thought… Let me clarify, I cared what others thought but not at the same level as the 1.0 version did. The 1.0 version would focusing on making sure I was meeting the needs of all others before putting my needs first. This had a different impact on many of my relationships, and I for the first time I didn't really care what others thought. I was happy and enjoying life. The 2.0 version felt so much more joy and happiness and was finally at peace.

Conclusion

Anybody can do anything they want, they must remove the word "can't" from their vocabulary and make a choice to figure it out. Money is empowering. Disability starts in the mind. The mind programs more than what we think. Health is very important. When you feel healthy you will do more. Health challenges always slow you down. You are your best teacher and your best student. Listen and teach yourself new challenging habits. I have learned from examples provided in my family life, that when you serve others and give back, you become so much "more." The Lions Club is a service-based organization that believes in giving back in several avenues.

I also have found that when I give of my time, I find new energy. To be involved in a service organization is empowering. The Lion's Club has provided me this experience, in my journey. When you step up and serve in whatever service organization, you not only grow but you provide the example for others to grow too. My hope is that everyone finds their purpose in life.

So, are you ready to Step Up and Grow?

www.ingramcontent.com/pod-product-compliance
Lightning Source LLC
Chambersburg PA
CBHW032107080426
42733CB00006B/456